1995 Raoul Wallenberg Lecture

COLLEGE OF ARCHITECTURE + URBAN PLANNING
THE UNIVERSITY OF MICHIGAN

Second Edition

© 1995 The University of Michigan

College of Architecture + Urban Planning

& Daniel Libeskind

Editor: Annette W. LeCuyer

Book Design: Christian Unverzagt

Images: with the cooperation of Elizabeth Govan / Studio Libeskind

Printing: Goetzcraft Printers, Inc., Ann Arbor

Printed and bound in the United States of America

Typeset in Monotype Baskerville and Futura Book

ISBN 0 9614792 1 3

The University of Michigan

College of Architecture + Urban Planning

2000 Bonisteel Boulevard

Ann Arbor, Michigan

48109-2069

USA

Daniel Libeskind
traces of the unborn

foreword

Raoul Wallenberg, who graduated from the College of Architecture and Urban Planning at the University of Michigan in 1935, has been called one of the century's most outstanding heroes. In 1944, as First Secretary of the Swedish legation in Budapest, he is credited with saving more than 100,000 Jews from death at the hands of the Nazis. The following year, Wallenberg was captured by the Russians. His fate is not known, although rumors persist that he is held in Russia even today.

To honor and remember this outstanding alumnus, Sol King, a former classmate of Wallenberg's, initiated the Wallenberg lecture series in 1971. In 1976, an endowment was established to ensure that an annual lecture be offered in Raoul's honor to focus on architecture as a humane social art. Since that series began, we have been honored to have at the college a number of distinguished speakers: Nikolaus Pevsner, Rudolf Arnheim, Joseph Rykwert, Spiro Kostof, Denise Scott Brown, James Marston Fitch, Joseph Esherick, and many more.

In inaugurating the Raoul Wallenberg Lectures, University President Robben W. Fleming cited the importance of celebrating the nobility of the human spirit. Such nobility is an attribute to which we all aspire, but which few of us ever find the courage, the intelligence and the fortitude to achieve. As a university, we cherish the self-image of being a citadel of the human spirit. This lecture annually honors an individual whose legendary acts of compassion exemplify the power of an individual to make a difference. Keeping the memory of his acts of compassion alive for generations of students and teachers alike, and celebrating architecture as a humane social art are the goals of this lecture series. I am delighted to welcome the architect Daniel Libeskind as the 1995 Raoul Wallenberg Lecturer.

Brian Carter
Professor & Chairman of Architecture

introduction

Daniel Libeskind's biography is so full of accolades and achievements that even a brief selection would give a good idea of the distinction of this architect. However, it is important to draw out some aspects of his life and work which may not be familiar but which serve to present the man Daniel Libeskind in a more comprehensive light.

It is well-known that he graduated from Cooper Union in architecture. Less known is that he studied and performed music, and relinquished a career as a concert pianist at the age of fifteen before turning to architecture. He went on to the University of Essex after Cooper Union for a post-graduate degree in the history and theory of architecture. That particular combination of disciplines bears on his broad knowledge and is, of course, endemic in his work.

It is widely known that Daniel Libeskind taught architecture at the Cranbrook Academy of the Arts; it is perhaps less known that he subsequently founded his own school in Milan and, for three years, continued to educate in his own format in a non-profit organization. It is unnecessary to mention that Daniel Libeskind has been a visiting professor and has lectured at many—if not all—of the illustrious universities world-wide. Less known is the fact that he is a guest professor at the obscure Academy an der Weissensee in former East Berlin, a school struggling to survive the economic and political changes in Germany.

Libeskind's exhibited work populates the collective memory of our discipline and his publications populate our personal libraries. His credits include a long list of distinguished awards and projects: the great machines in the 1985 Venice Biennale, the City Edge project that won first prize in the IBA in 1987, and the first prize for the extension to the Berlin Museum in 1989. In that same year Libeskind was offered a Senior

Fellowship at the Getty Foundation, the first architect to have this honor bestowed upon him. He declined that position to move to Berlin in order to ensure the future of the Berlin Museum extension, his first major built work. Of all the acclaim that this unfinished work has received, it is perhaps most telling that the German Akademie der Künste, an institution hardly known for it openness to the *avant garde*, has found it irresistible to embrace Libeskind as a member.

Finally, while Daniel Libeskind continues to inspire with his architectural genius, equally inspiring is the tactical genius of his wife and partner Nina Libeskind, whose tireless contributions to the work of Studio Libeskind must not go unrecognized. On behalf of the college, I would like to cordially welcome both Daniel and Nina Libeskind.

Kent Kleinman
Assistant Professor of Architecture

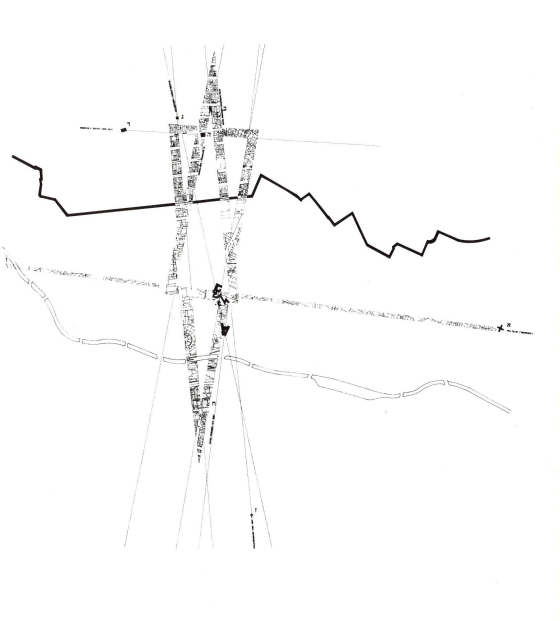

traces of the unborn

I thank the college for the invitation to speak here, and particularly for the opportunity of addressing this humanitarian theme in honor of Raoul Wallenberg. It is important for us as architects and planners to see in Wallenberg what nobility really means: the courage, in the face of incredible adversity and hopelessness, to perform acts which are deeply human. Wallenberg's deeds affected not only the thousands of people who were saved, but the millions of others who now carry the theme of Raoul Wallenberg with them. His was clearly the life of a man who was dedicated to truth.

I am not prepared to make an explicit connection here, but in architecture there are also forces which apply pressure from left and right, and it is difficult to remain on course. It is difficult to see the human, ethical perspective in various projects and involvements as an architect. The contemporary era is one of tremendous change in architecture and in the politics of space. Particularly having come recently from Germany, I am aware of the change from the European perspective. Nostalgia for the past—an idea of returning to something that might have been but can no longer be—is instrumental in distorting and deforming modernity and the quest for an ever-better spiritual and architectural situation of human beings. Of course, that is true globally. As the economic pressures come, one must resist the temptation to become a victim of easy ideologies which tend to flatten and reduce architectural discourse through, very often, underlying authoritarian agendas. Those authoritarian agendas might be expressed in different ways in different parts of the world. It is therefore important for us to be aware of the legacy of someone like Wallenberg, a unique individual who never faltered in his belief that human beings are always capable of doing a little bit better.

I have selected several projects which I am pursuing in which I myself struggle to keep on course between political, social, & architectural extremes and to produce something which has significance to people. The three projects which I have selected represent in some way the panorama, I would call it, of my own architectural commitment.

The first project is for the former Sachsenhausen SS-lands which today lie as a main site in the city of Oranienburg. This project is derived from my own conscious decision to reject a given competition program. I was invited to participate in a competition and, after thinking about it, could not execute the political demand of that particular project. I thought that the project could be done in another way, and I was committed to seeing it done in another way.

The second project is an urban proposal for Alexanderplatz which represents my commitment to demonstrate a new idea of urban design which is neither a capitulation to the erasure of history nor the temptation to repeat history once again.

The third project is the Jewish Museum in Berlin which represents the architectural and political struggle to get a building built. I do not have to tell you that the easiest part of such a project is to win a competition—to make drawings, to make models, to think, to meditate, to invent new possibilities. The most difficult task, as I think I have learned from my wife and partner Nina, is the struggle to go to the next step—to implement such plans, to get them built, and to get public support for such a project. That has been a struggle. The competition was launched in 1988 before the Wall came down and was judged in 1989 after the Wall came down. The realization has taken many years. Now the building is well underway and will open in a very short time. The struggle to go beyond simply the drawn is a huge commitment.

sachsenhausen

A few years ago, I was involved in a competition for urbanization of the former SS-lands in Oranienburg, about 40 kilometers from Berlin. This is a very important site because Sachsenhausen, founded in 1933, was the first concentration camp to be built in history. It was built by architects of the Beaux Arts tradition. There were many architects involved; this was not a minor project. It was done to symbolize the inhumanity, the unreason, and the hell of the regime of the Third Reich. It was in fact a model of what such a camp would look like if it were to be representative. It was purportedly not a death camp, but the prisoners were put to death through hard labor. The first gas chambers were not in Poland, they were in Germany and existed at Sachsenhausen in a strongly emblematic form. I had read about Sachsenhausen before and thought it was somewhere far away, but it is right in the center of Oranienburg in the state of Brandenburg. The competition called for urbanizing the site with massive housing estates. I thought about urbanization—the need to bring life back to the centers of cities—which is a critical issue in the lands of former East Germany. I felt that, although I risked disqualification—which indeed happened—I could not propose the 10,000 units of housing requested.

Today, the entire site is both a memorial and a wasteland. The camp as a whole was built as an idealized city of death, divided into two by an enormous gate, with the victims inside and the perpetrators of the crimes outside. It occupied hundreds of acres of land and was structured in a perfect triangular plan. The triangle is more than just an emblem in plan. It was the sign of all of the prisoners. There were hundreds of thousands of prisoners in the camp. Each wore a different colored triangle—the homosexuals, the Jehovah's Witnesses, the French, the Resistance, and people who believed in the Bible. Jews wore the double triangle.

The gateway was at the center, with the concentration camp and gas chambers to the north. The SS facilities were to the south outside of the gate and included halls where the SS lived, garages where the equipment for torture was kept, and the whole infrastructure for the running of the camp mechanism. To the west, adjacent to the main road to the center of Oranienburg, is a key T-shaped building which was the headquarters of Himmler, the commandant of the SS. Today, strangely, it is a restored administration building for the city; it was built by slave labor and yet is an important public place. I proposed to integrate it into the entire project. To the east is the Villa Eiche, which was the residence of the camp commandant.

I thought it was absurd to propose 10,000 units of housing for such a site. The program also called for re-use of all the buildings. Many of them are now in dilapidated condition, but they were to be re-used as kindergartens, social facilities, and office buildings. I could not accept such a proposition, and as a result, I was disqualified from the competition. However, I received a special award. The judges said that it was good that I had reminded them of the history of the camp. A housing project won the first award, and we struggled against it by continuing to work on the project and showing it to the citizens of Oranienburg. Over a long period of time, the people of the town and the government of Oranienburg began to see the project differently. They began to see that housing might not be the best way to bring people to the site. Just recently, we were very happy to learn that the parliament of Oranienburg had reversed the decision by deciding to implement this particular concept for the site instead of building housing.

The camp was built on axiality. My proposal cuts the site of the camp and tilts the entire orientation of the camp away from the central axis at a particular latitude which goes through Lubeck. Lubeck was associated with an infamous death march. At the end of the war in 1945, thousands of prisoners were marched from Sachsenhausen because there were no more possibilities for exterminating them. They were to be marched to Lubeck to be drowned in a big ship. They never made it because the convoy was bombed. The number of deaths and the route of that convoy are emblematic of the late twentieth century and important for the twenty-first century. After the war the history of the camp continued. The site was used by the Soviet troops and the East German STASI, and it continued to have evil functions on it, not only prisons but also spilling of oil and other forms of pollution.

I have therefore denied the centrality of the former axis of the camp with a new topography. Around this conversion of the landscape, I proposed to bring water to part of the site and to rebuild the polluted land. I proposed to intervene on a larger ecological basis in terms of water, land, and the topography of the town. It is important to reveal explicitly the connection between new activities and the history of the place and not to obliterate or make banal the history of this land.

I proposed what I call the 'hope incision', a very controlled cut into the landscape with a completely new topography and a new way of dealing ecologically with the land. Rather than housing, I proposed to bring new activities to the site which are badly needed in this part of the city: places for those who do not have employment; places where those who do not have skills can be educated; places of an ecumenical nature; social facilities such as libraries; and a badly needed archive for the town. Places were proposed for redeveloping crafts which had been obliterated by the GDR regime. For example, the town was famous in the past for making musical instruments.

One part of the site, this park of ruins as I call it, would explicitly thematize the connection of the entire infrastructure and land formation with the history of the camp. It would also look toward a new future for the town, bringing people here in a considered way, not in a careless way. Half of the site is to be physically transformed and landscaped into a place of ruin and water, showing the already ruined former SS barracks and their connection to history. The barracks are to be brought into the social program of the hope incision, of the memorial, and of the new public space. I did not agree with the competition program that the SS facilities should be reconstructed and re-used. I thought they should slowly fall into decay and proposed how such a thing could be controllable architecturally. It is not easy to make buildings fall into oblivion over time because one has to control that process, but I am working on it.

The other half of the vast site is to be landscaped with new trees, new vegetation, and is to have a light intervention of commerce, craft and education. There are to be certain connections between various buildings, traces of the past, and traces of future history which are linked together in a much larger whole.

At present, the entrance to the camp is along the side. I suggested that it should be returned to its original position the main axis. A new entrance is proposed around the deformed and dispossessed Villa Eiche which was considered by the competition organizers to be an important and beautiful building. I saw no aesthetic beauty in it; it was built only to look impressive. I have proposed to transform it into the library with its entrance along the main route in and out of Oranienburg.

This is a prototypical theme: how to use lands which are not fully profane. I would call them semi-profane. They are lands which cannot be treated normally because they are in an in-between state. The problem of function and the site revolves around the need to reveal its history while at the same time creating a place for hope and new activity without domestication of violence. It is important to deal with the site and not to obliterate its history. Of the seven architects in the competition, six saw fit to plant trees and make fountains here in accordance with the program and to deny the fact that the town's history is implicated and must also go on in the future. I thought that these connections, for new generations who never had direct experience of the camp and who were born in a new time, should not be ambiguous, but should be structured architecturally and in terms of planning both as a memory and as a productive future.

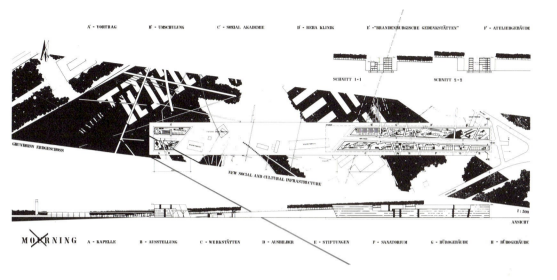

One has to think of course of how to implement such a plan. There were many critics saying, "We cannot bring all the water in. It is impossible cost-wise." I therefore considered how to transform the relationships and how to bring the water to the site in a different way via canals. I also expanded the scheme because the town said they needed twice as much development to take place on the land. I continued to work with the authorities and the historians who insisted that some buildings be kept. I agreed finally that if the buildings were not simply to be obliterated for domestic use, that if they would return to the memorial as functions of public space, some of them could be kept. I have worked continuously with the conceptual and architectural ideas to make the proposal a reality.

Again I have to give the credit to my partner and wife Nina. When the competition result was announced, I gave up, thinking that there was no way to convince the town that they had made the wrong decision. By working together, I learned that one should never give up. Instead one should try to meet people on another level. We presented the project to people who were not part of the government, just normal people. They began to see, particularly the young people who were educated in the DDR system, that they were not aware of the history of the site. It was amazing. Several historians came to me and said, "Mr. Libeskind, we never knew about it." This is not a domestic site. The importance of reversing the competition decision is the acknowledgement that the banality of the domestic does not really have a role in urbanizing the image and function of the town, and of this camp.

alexanderplatz

The second work is a large urban project, quite different in its scope. Alexanderplatz was the main center of Berlin, the old center. When the unification of Germany came, and with it the unification of Berlin, Alexanderplatz came back to the fore as the center of the city. What should one do with such a place and where does one turn for inspiration? Alexanderplatz has been completely transformed since the 1930s when the famous schemes by Mies van der Rohe, the Luckhardt brothers, Behrens, Poelzig, and Mendelsohn were proposed. Many famous architects worked on this site during the twenties and thirties but nothing much materialized because history took another course. Now, another surprise turn of history has come with the unification of Berlin.

I turned to a doctor for information about the site. Alfred Doblin was a famous writer, the James Joyce of Berlin. However, few people know that he was a medical doctor who had his practice in East Berlin near Alexanderplatz. He studied Alexanderplatz from a medical point of view in the twenties and thirties. To paraphrase, he said, "When I stand on Alexanderplatz, I am in East Berlin." This was an amazing thing to say in 1920 before the war and before the Wall. He said, " I am in East Berlin because this is where the people are. In West Berlin are the zoo, the Kufurstendamm, and very nice houses." He used those categories, East and West. This view is still correct, although the delineations of space have changed.

Doblin was asked how he would describe Alexanderplatz. He made an imprint of his left hand and said, "That is Alexanderplatz." I meditated on this fascinating act. Why wasn't it his right hand? Why was it his left hand? Was it about left architecture versus right architecture? Was it about fascism and leftist ideology? Was it about the fact that the invisible lines of the hand which are an occult and palmistic destiny of the body, are themselves never visible when the hand grasps the tools of work? All of these thoughts coagulated in my mind as a strategy for looking at Alexanderplatz, and for deciphering its history, which is not an easy task to do today.

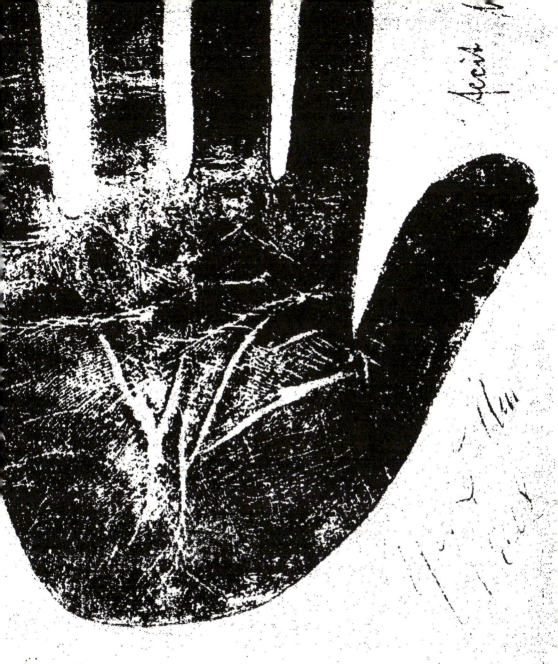

main, die Hand. Alfred Döblin studiert die Linien mit
l sagt: „Sicher ist mir nur, daß es die linke Hand ist."

This part of the city was named when Czar Alexander came into Berlin in
the eighteenth century, and it remained Alexanderplatz when the Russian
troops departed from exactly the same spot in 1989. In the 1930s the space was
formed by two Behrens buildings in a huge, very dense population quarter.
Alexanderplatz today looks very different. It is difficult to orient oneself because
so little remains from the past, except an invisible linkage to the Doblinian
interpretation. There are new buildings, and a new scale.

The incredible idea of demolishing the city is unique to Berlin. Streets in
other cities of the world such as Paris, New York and London seem to be sacred
territory; nobody changes the street patterns in most cities of the world. This
is not the case in Berlin. Berlin has always had the idea that if a house can
be removed, the direction or course of a street can also be changed. There
have been hundreds of proposals for changing street patterns in Berlin. It is
poignant to realize that the ideas of devastating the city predated the physical
destruction of Alexanderplatz during the war, before all the utopian schemes of
the great modernists had appeared in the periodicals, much less been completed.

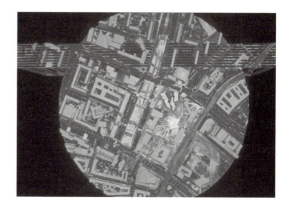

Even though this competition took place in a particular city in Europe, there were certain fundamental points that I wanted to address which relate to issues of other urban centers, whether the devastation is because of war, political catastrophe, or economic catastrophe as in American cities. I thought of the axiom of Paul Valéry, one of my favorite philosophers and poets, who said, "Humanity is permanently threatened by two dangers: order and disorder." The threat comes from left and right, from order and disorder. I have tried to make a scheme which navigates between this Scylla and Charybdis of nostalgic historicism on the one hand, and of the *tabula rasa* of a totalitarian kind of thinking on the other.

The competition was in two stages with 18 international architects. I was lucky to win the second prize with a scheme which is diametrically opposed to the winning scheme. Even though only one vote separates the two schemes, there is an abyss in the understanding of urban space. The winning scheme proposes 50 skyscrapers of equal height standing on a Cartesian grid, each built of granite. They are all the same, each with an Art Deco top. I could not understand this approach. I proposed a scheme which follows the history of Alexanderplatz and emphatically rejects the idea of isolating once again the urban problem from the social and political problem by building, for example, isolated islands of office buildings. I reject the idea that totalitarian planning can still be engaged in the late twentieth century. I do not think that the city can be demolished yet again. My proposal calls for immediate interaction of the existing with the new, with the possible. I proposed to supplement and to alter, but to deal with what is there today. I suggested to the investors of the competition that they need not demolish a set of buildings in order to rebuild them once again in another style. The alternative is to simply improve them for now. None of us knows what 'for now' really means.

My approach is not very popular in Berlin political circles. In view of Berlin politics today, these buildings do not really exist. All of the other architects in the competition proposed that ideally, during the next forty years, all existing buildings will be demolished. I am not a fan of East German architecture and I do not think that it has much merit architecturally, but this is not a question of aesthetics. The issue is the displacement of tens of thousands of people who have lived on this site for fifty years. This housing was built as a showcase for the DDR regime. This was the best housing, the best place to live. The radical feature of my idea in view of Berlin politics is to advocate the acceptance of the existence of these vast housing estates, and to accept the fact that people live there, that their lives have to be bettered, and that these lives have a memory of at least two generations. Even the prefabricated and ill-conceived buildings of the former DDR, which have little architectural merit, should not be singled out for demolition. This is an important point: Planning and architecture should not condone demolition; they should deal with construction and the incorporation of difficult conditions in a new and ecologically responsible manner.

I propose not to alter traffic routes, not to engage in new street design, but to re-use all existing streets in a different way. The huge Karl Marx Allee goes from Alexanderplatz through the Schoeneberg residential quarter to all the outlying

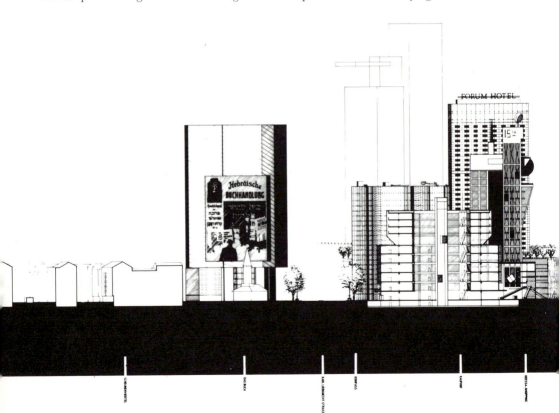

areas. I did not monumentalize the Karl Marx Allee as the other competitors did. I proposed to build a series of pavilions in the median to provide facilities badly needed by the nearby housing estates—recreation facilities, inexpensive movie theaters and restaurants, sports facilities, and so on. One must deal with the thousands of people who are living here and provide facilities which mediate between the old part of the city and the residential areas. This goes against the grain today. Today, Berliners are talking about renaming Karl Marx Allee to become Friedrich Hegel Allee. I think that, better than renaming streets, is to do what Hegel would have done: to mediate the dialectic extremes of east and west, good and bad, and various aesthetics by participation.

In the scheme which I designed, the old buildings on the site—the big Forum Hotel, the huge buildings of the newspaper *Berliner Zeitung*, the old Kaufhof department store—are to be retained. The site is to be opened emphatically with a new wedge building. This building is to serve a public function as the European information focal point for Berlin, particularly for the people from the East. My only intervention in Alexanderplatz itself is to provide a bigger entrance and exit to the underground. The underground system is one of the few things which remains intact from the Berlin of the 1920s. The shape of the wedge building exactly matches a gigantic, ominous bunker under Alexanderplatz which is closed to the public. I propose that the bunker should become a public place which is part of the vertical circulation linking the underground exits and entrances to Alexanderplatz. I refuse to orient my scheme from the viewpoint of the western portal because I believe that the majority of people will see another view, as I did when I came to Berlin as a child from Poland. Alfred Doblin or anybody coming from the East arrived at Alexanderplatz station, and not at the zoo or the Kufurstendamm. The eastern gateway to Berlin must be reinforced.

ALEX

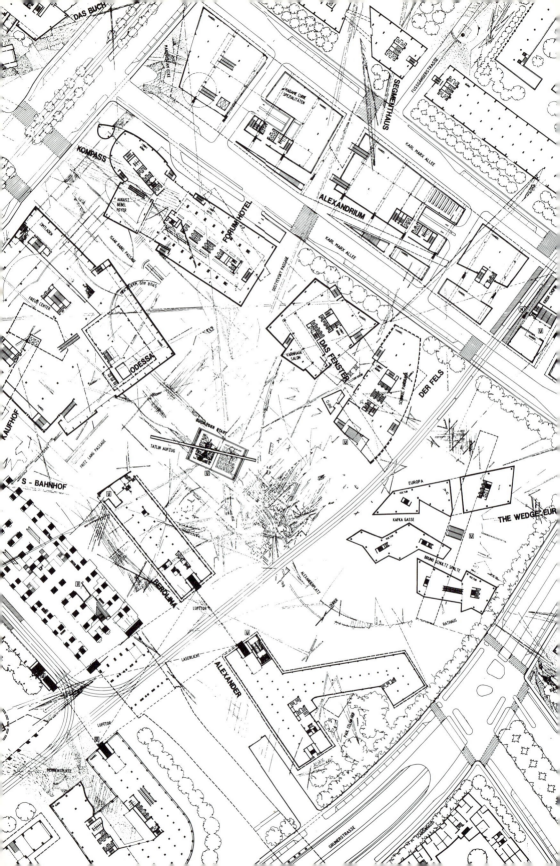

Oddly, everyone else in the competition did away with the existing buildings like the Kaufhof and the Forum Hotel. Investors have already poured more than 60 million Marks into the renovation of these buildings. I do not think that the investors plan on destroying these buildings in the next five years. Perhaps they will be demolished in thirty years. It depends on how Europe develops and how Berlin will fare. In my view, it is important for the existing tall buildings to be incorporated, and I have therefore suggested a contextual re-reading of the site. The site has the old height of Berlin as represented by the Behrens buildings, but it has also the intermediate height of the proposed Mendelsohn, Mies van der Rohe, and Luckhardt buildings, and the new height of the television tower, the Forum Hotel, and other big buildings. The Kaufhof building was the most successful department store of the Eastern Bloc. People told me, "Please Mr. Libeskind, leave something that we can remember on this site." I proposed to keep the Kaufhof, to double the area of the store, and to bring it up to date with new elevator cores. I proposed a new open air tower, the Odessa Tower, with inexpensive rental spaces for markets which happen here frequently.

The re-working and particularly the transparency of spaces leading out of and into Alexanderplatz are important. The obsession in Berlin today, as in many other places, is to bring history back. The award-winning scheme says that Alexanderplatz will look like Piazza Navona. I thought that it will never look like Piazza Navona. It should not look like Piazza Navona. It cannot look like Piazza Navona because underneath Alexanderplatz, there is a transportation system like 42nd Street and Times Square which can bring three million people to this place every fifteen minutes. The image of reverie of the past is inappropriate. The Berlin of tomorrow is a place of tumultuous activity and of functional connections to both existing and new buildings.

I have also proposed a linear park, which was not a part of the competition program, to connect the East with the Spree throughout all of these ruins of ideologies. It is important to understand that these sites are already owned by investors. The architecture is already made for these places. This is a planning competition to decide what is the nature of—and I would say emphatically— the *public space*, not the private space of the offices, and how to connect the public space in the vertical and horizontal dimensions.

I made a model at 1:2000 scale as required by the competition, but I thought one should also look at the site at 1:500 scale. One should see every window and one should ask the people what they think. Should the windows move a little bit? Is this a good idea? Should the buildings be lower or higher? Should one see something else? I proposed to the Senate of Berlin to bring the citizens into the

full participatory process. Particularly with contemporary technologies, there is no reason why the public cannot participate in making decisions about planning. That did not endear me with the planners of Berlin.

I believe that the idea of the totality, the finality of the masterplan is misguided. One should advocate a gradual transformation of public space, a metamorphic process, without relying on a hypothetical time in the future when everything will be perfect. The mistake of planners and architects is to believe that fifty years from now Alexanderplatz will be perfected. We see this same illusion demonstrated over and over on Alexanderplatz. The time is now. The interaction is now.

One should not see cities as pathological entities, as being sick. One should see them as needing care. What is needed, in my view, is a Buddhist or homeopathic approach to city planning comprised of gentle interventions, which are not very dramatic in terms of instant gratification. I tried to tell people, particularly in the west, that there is nothing wrong with Alexanderplatz. It is an incredible place which is pregnant with possibilities that have not yet been played out. That is true of many cities. My picture postcard of Berlin says, "Wish you were here." The competition jury may have selected a group of identical skyscrapers standing in a rigid grid, all of equal height, all of granite. Without winning the competition, I think I have shown how Berlin will actually develop. It must develop this way because the alternative is hopeless.

The city is the greatest artistic and spiritual creation of human beings. It is a collective work which exists not only in space but also in time. Its structure is intrinsically mysterious. Let me put it this way: When you see Alexanderplatz or the city, it is more like a dream than like the construction of a washing machine or a car. In this sense, I have tried to propose an alternative to the whole notion of the masterplan with its implied idea of totality, of finality, and the misguided ambition which I think all plans have of the eternal recurrence of the same through replication of type and through replication of order. I think we know this is a nihilistic notion. I propose instead a process which reinforces the structure of change in a heterogeneous, pluralistic and diverse architecture. In a democratic society, one should acknowledge that architecture will reflect very different, and sometimes conflicting views of the world. This is an alternative approach to the traditional idea of planning which implies continuity based on projection. It is an approach which treats the city as an evolving poetic and unpredictable structure.

the jewish museum

In 1989, after we had gone to Berlin to collect the prize for winning the competition, my wife Nina turned to me and said, "We cannot leave. If we are serious about the competition, we have to stay in Berlin." Of course, that was true. We moved to Berlin.

The competition was done in 1988 and judged in 1989. The program was for an extension to the Berlin Museum to house collections relating to Jewish history and culture. My idea was that the one thing that unifies Berlin is the connection of Berliners and Jews, not East and West ideologies. I located my project across the Wall, believing that the issue which can connect Berlin to itself across ideological boundaries is its connection to its Jewish citizens, who were exterminated by the hundreds of thousands in that city and by the millions in the world.

I constructed the project on a connection between addresses east and west, and names, and places which would implode themselves on the particular site of the museum across a tremendous void, across an abyss which is the Holocaust. This was an event across which no connection of an obvious kind can ever be made again. I used an emblematic and distorted matrix of the Star of David which, to me, did not shine with address, but with the absence of address. I used various methods—geometric, architectural, planning, and political—to make a tectonic intervention in Berlin.

The Museum is not just a building but is part of the city. The site can be seen on the Baroque map of Berlin near to the Brandenburg Gate, Pariser Platz, Leipziger Platz, Potsdamer Platz, and the Rondel. The Berlin Museum is on axis with the Gendarmenmarkt by Schinkel, and the site is adjacent to the existing Museum. The Baroque building for the museum was destroyed during the war and was completely rebuilt in the sixties. Nearby is a building of Erich Mendelsohn who had to leave Berlin because he was a Jew. The street patterns were changed by Scharoun's plan. There are nineteenth century buildings mixed with some of the massive post-war projects. To the south and the east are the new projects of IBA, the international building exposition of the late

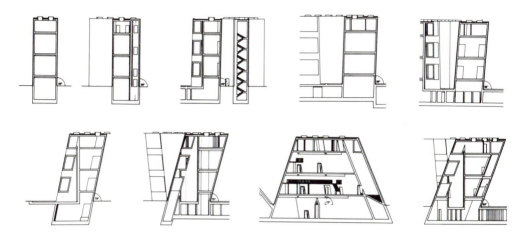

seventies and eighties. In 1988, the Berlin Wall still went through the entire area. This site is an emblem of the diversity, of the fatality, and of the optimism of the kind of accelerated history of which Berlin is uniquely representative. The city was destroyed and has arisen, destined again to play an important role in the culture of cities and of the world. The site itself mirrors in its evolution, its history, its erasure, and its continual turmoil the program of the museum.

The program of the museum is how to bring this history together, how not to isolate the Jewish history from the history of Berlin, how not to turn the Jewish history into some anthropological specimen of an absence. The museum must show how Berlin and its Jews are inextricably connected in their past, in their fatality, and in the destiny of their future. This city had 200,000 Jewish citizens, not all as famous as Arnold Schoenberg, Albert Einstein, Walter Benjamin, or Max Reinhardt, but thousands of people who worked in industry, cinema, theater, and business. The task of this project is to show this history. It is no ordinary museum.

There are three fundamental concepts on which the museum is based: First is that it is impossible to understand the history of Berlin without understanding the enormous intellectual, economic and cultural contribution of the Jewish citizens of Berlin. Second is the physical and spiritual necessity to integrate the significance of the Holocaust into the building. The Holocaust was not merely

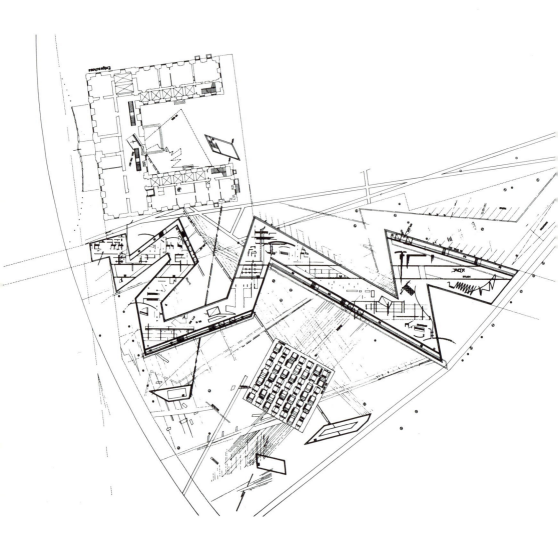

an event in history, but an altering axial event in the memory of Berlin. Third is to express how, through the acknowledgement of a particular form of absence, life can have meaning and an optimistic, hopeful direction.

Programmatically, the competition required that the Baroque building remain as the entrance to the entire museum complex. I proposed that the museum and its new extension should stand separate. There is no bridge or surface connection between the two buildings. The connection is underground, through the Baroque foundations of the Berlin Museum. A series of independent buildings is placed around an empty space which is the orienting feature, a building buried within a building. The void runs through the building but is invisible from the outside and only accessible via bridges. It is the underground introduction to the history of Berlin.

From the entrance in the Baroque Berlin Museum, three roads lead the visitor into the new museum. One road represents the extermination of not only hundreds of thousands of Berliners, but also of would-be Berliners such as the Polish Jews who came to Berlin. This road represents the end of Berlin as we knew it, the apocalyptic void. I proposed to the Senate of Berlin that the tower of the Holocaust should exhibit a single transformation of how the signature of the Berliner changed to a number and then to the last signature. The last signatures of all Berliners exist in the archives—hundreds of thousands of them— and I want to use them in a special way to try to break through the statistical idea of the Holocaust which is unfathomable. Who can understand the millions and what it meant? The Holocaust tower is dedicated to the understanding of a singular transformation. It is not a fully profane part of the museum; it is semi-profane.

The second road, which crosses the first, represents the exile and emigration of Berliners. So many Berliners are elsewhere—in New York, Sydney, Tel Aviv, and even Ann Arbor. I spoke yesterday in Ann Arbor with Professor Arnheim who is a Berliner. This road of exile and emigration leads to a very special garden which I call the E.T.A. Hoffmann Garden. Hoffmann was the romantic writer of incredible tales, and I dedicated this garden to him because he was a lawyer working in a building adjacent to the site. The connection of the law and the court to the concept of the building is very important. The garden is on an oblique plane tilted toward the underground exile emigration route and is composed of 48 columns filled with earth in which the vegetation grows in an inverse way: it grows down. I had originally thought that all columns would be clad in Jerusalem stone. Now, perhaps only the forty-ninth column will be clad in that way. The garden represents 1948, the year of the formation of the state of Israel and what exile, emigration, and foundation might mean from the perspective of the integrity of Jewish Berlin culture.

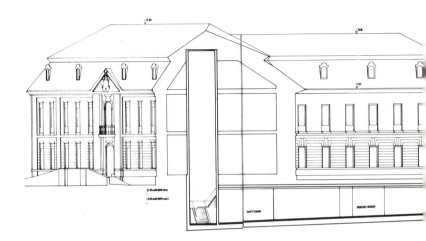

The longest and straightest road in the underground matrix is the road
leading to the main circulation stair up to the fragile, vulnerable continuity
of the history of Berlin across the abyss. This is the introduction to the Berlin
of today and tomorrow.

The entrance to the new building is very deep, more than ten metres under the
foundations of the Baroque building. From the entrance, one is faced with three
roads: the road leading to the Holocaust tower which is windowless and has no
entrance except from the underground level; the road leading to the garden; and
the road leading to the main circulation stair and the void. The entire plane of
the museum is tilted toward the void of the superstructure. The building is as
complex as the history of Berlin.

Although the program originally called for a chronological display, I have
introduced the idea of the void as a physical interference with chronology.
The void is the one element of continuity throughout the complex form of the
building. It is 22 metres high and runs the entire length of the building, over
140 metres. It is a straight line whose impenetrability forms the central axis.
The void is traversed by bridges which connect the various parts of the museum
to each other. The scheme is really seven independent buildings which are
seemingly unified into one building because they are all related in the same
way to the bridges. The void, or absence, will be experienced by every
participant going through the collections of the history of Berlin. It is accessible

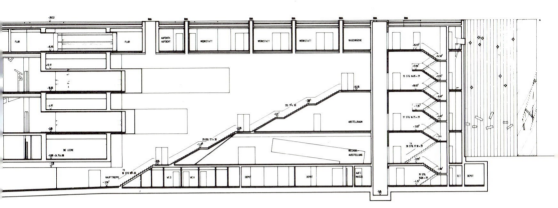

only from the religious collections of the Jewish community of Berlin which date back to the thirteenth century. I thought this should be the only place where one could see the dimension of the void. Of course, one can never see the complete significance of the absence, even from the underground position. The building is built in the same way as it is conceptually constructed in that the bridges are the last thing to be put into the building. They are the lightweight elements, and only when they are installed will one be able to walk through the different fragments in a unified way.

The void and the invisible are the structural features which I have gathered in this particular space of Berlin and exposed in architecture. The experience of the building is organized around a center which is not to be found in any explicit way because it is not visible. In terms of this museum, what is not visible is the richness of the former Jewish contribution to Berlin. It cannot be found in artifacts because it has been turned to ash. It has physically disappeared. This is part of the exhibit: a museum where no museological functions can actually take place.

Light and the kinetic experience of the body are translated through the windows of the museum. Although this may sound intellectual or complex, the museum is meant to be experienced by people who have never read about the Holocaust or who do not know much about it. The task of the museum is to introduce light to the body in a corporeal way—to the legs and to the feet, so to speak.

The building is about moving through light. The light is a peculiar and special light which falls into the museum toward the absent space of the void, and then into the bridge which connects to the next part of the museum.

The function of the bridges in terms of exhibits is to double everything in the museum. Everything in Berlin has double meaning. If the paintings of Max Liebermann are exhibited, they cannot be exhibited as paintings from one side only. One has to see their other side. Their other side is the desperate letters of Liebermann's wife writing to the Chief of the Gestapo saying that she is the wife of the most famous painter in Berlin and that she should be released from Auschwitz. She never succeeded. The other side of the writings of Walter Benjamin, who wrote the greatest guidebooks to Berlin, is the suicide note he wrote in Spain while trying to escape the Nazis and the missing manuscript of *The Messiah*. The other side of the Schoenberg *Moses and Aaron* score is the rhythm of the void.

There are other conceptual constructs that I have used in the museum. First is the irrationality of the matrix of connection which has to do with the light, with the connection of address and the erasure of address, and with the connection across the city today. Second are the two different building sections: through the buildings and through the void itself. The void is always symmetrical. There are always left and right doorways which look the same. The building is symmetrical in its transverse section, but completely asymmetrical in its longitudinal section. Third is my interest in Schoenberg, particularly in his incompletable opera *Moses and Aaron* in which he deals with the problem of Berlin. It is not an unfinished opera; it is incompletable in musical terms because of the relationship between Moses and Aaron. I have sought to complete the Act III libretto in architectural form in the rhythm of the void. The fourth element that I have used to structure the museum is the *Einbahnstrasse* text by Walter Benjamin. The text did not help me to design the museum. To the contrary, the museum is a mechanism to interpret the text, that is, to open up the thinking of the one-way street as he called it. I used the sixty stations in the text of Benjamin as the apocalyptic encounter between lines of light and stations on the distorted Star of David. The fifth element is my interest in names, addresses and numbers associated with the deported Berliners. I started with only six, then twelve, then thirty-six, but I am into the thousands now. This work does not end with the building of the museum. I can only claim a small credit for this building, for it is really the ideas of Schoenberg and Benjamin, of those anonymous addressees and addresses, and of those deported people who, in their absence, are present in Berlin.

It is easy to say 'space of the void' on a drawing, but when it is cubic metres and it costs money and the client is paying for building walls, then one must communicate the importance of the absence of that space as part of the museum concept. It took a long time, but I did communicate the idea, not just to important historians and philosophers of architecture, but to the people of Berlin. I was fortunate to find resonance and understanding. This building, just like any building, went through tremendous birth pangs. It was not an easy building for the city to build, not because of its geometry or its architecture, but because of what it represents in terms of its exhibition. Much more is at stake than the architecture of the building. The absence, which has been cut off in history, is also the bridge to the future of Berlin. It is through that absence that Berlin goes on. What does it all mean in terms of concrete, in terms of windows, and in terms of financial restrictions? How does one take it all on as part of the project?

The elevations are literal inscriptions of the conceptual constructs running through the dimensions of fatality and hope. The incisions are deliberate, systematic. The windows open in various arcs of disclosure. It is easy to talk about a concept, but to meet all of the stringent regulations, to pass all of the codes, and to keep the building on budget is more difficult. I am proud to report that the building is not even a pfennig over budget and is ahead of the

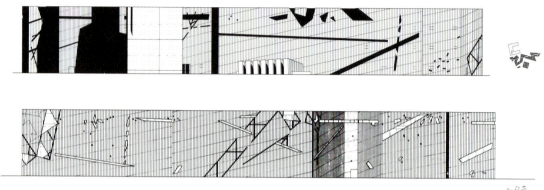

construction schedule. The topping out ceremonies marking the completion of the building volume will be on 5 May. It will take at least another 18 months to complete the finishes.

The building is a hybrid construction of steel and concrete. Some of the windows are hanging in apparently impossible configurations. The concrete is exposed only in the void. Elsewhere, because of the requirements of exhibitions, the concrete is clad. The building is a heterogeneous trajectory through religion, industry, art history, theater, film, fashion, literature, music, and many other areas of study. I have tried not to expose in any consistent manner any single trajectory in the building with regard to materials, organization, or even the distinction between the Berlin Museum and the Jewish Museum.

Externally, the building will be clad in zinc. I got the idea of using zinc from Schinkel. Before his very early death, he recommended that any young architect in Berlin should use as much zinc as possible. I thought that if Schinkel recommended this, I had better do it. In Berlin, untreated zinc turns to a beautiful blue-gray. Many of Schinkel's Berlin buildings, particularly at the Kleinglienicke Park, are built of zinc which has been painted white. When you knock them, you can tell that they are just covers. That is very Berlin-like.

Someone said to me, "Is this, Mr. Libeskind, how you learned to construct walls in school?" Sometimes architecture is not exactly as you have been taught. The concrete workers who are constructing the walls are from the Fischerbau company in southern Germany and are incredible. I can hardly read the formwork drawings, but they have no problem at all. They just look and say, "It is surprising we should be asked to do this. In thirty-five years in architecture, we have never been asked to exercise our skills in constructing such forms." They are not only ahead of schedule, but have been brought into the process. It is indicative that when the Senate opened the public sites to the people of Berlin, ten people went to Potsdamer Platz to look at the construction of corporate office buildings, but thousands of people came to the Jewish Museum. People are always interested in how a wall is made. In Berlin, people have a real interest in architecture.

Buildings are important. One can always put a book away. The testament of Raoul Wallenberg can be hidden, but a building and the city are always present across time, across history. The act of building itself transforms the culture of a city. People thought all sorts of things in the beginning, but as the museum has

become visible, I am happy to say that it has become a popular place. Of course, it is not yet open to the public but large groups have been through it. It seems to have a healing power through the tension between the forms of expression and its political content.

To conclude, the museum is about more than Berliners and Jews. It is about more than things of the past. These issues are important for all human beings. I am aware that my view of this building is from the inside of Berlin's Jewish history; I have never stepped out of it. I am a kind of Berliner. Ernst Reuter, in 1945 just after Berlin was liberated by the Allies, made the famous speech from the Brandenburg Gate, "Look to the world. We are the free Berlin." Years later Kennedy said, "Ich bin ein Berliner," and signalled that everyone had become a Berliner somehow.

I have sought to create a different architecture for a time which would reflect an understanding of history after world catastrophe. The Holocaust was the premonition, and of course Nagasaki and Hiroshima came soon after. I am also seeking a new understanding of what a museum is, an altered relationship between program, the function of architecture, and architectural form. The museum is not only a response to a particular program with a very specific intent, it is a new emblem of hope. It underscores the necessity to create a different— and by different I mean ethical—architecture for the twenty-first century which is based on a fundamentally transformed political, cultural, and spiritual experience of the twentieth century.

Daniel Libeskind
February 1995

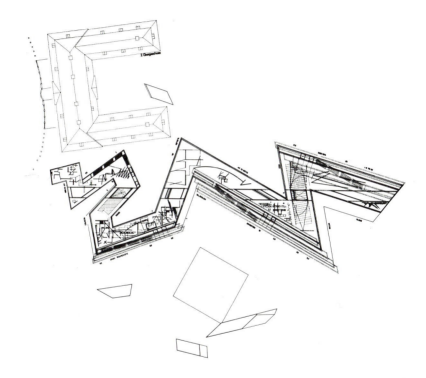

raoul wallenberg lecture

The Raoul Wallenberg Lecture was initiated in 1971 by Sol King, a former classmate of Wallenberg's. An endowment was established in 1976 for an annual lecture to be offered in Raoul's honor on the theme of architecture as a humane social art. The following distinguished architects and historians have been invited to present the Wallenberg lectures to the College of Architecture + Urban Planning at the University of Michigan:

1972 Sir Nikolaus Pevsner, C.B.E.
1973 Eric Larabee
1975 Reyner Banham
1976 Rudolf Arnheim
1978 Jacob B. Bakema
1979 James Marston Fitch
1981 Carl Levin
1983 Edmund Bacon
1984 Charles Correa
1985 Grady Clay
1987 Joseph Rykwert
1988 Spiro Kostof
1989 J. Max Bond, Jr.
1990 Elizabeth Hollander
1991 Joseph Esherick
1992 Denise Scott Brown
1993 James Ingo Freed
1994 Jorge Silvetti
1995 Daniel Libeskind

raoul wallenberg scholarship

The Raoul Wallenberg Scholarship is awarded through
a design competition which is held annually for
undergraduates in their final year of study in the
College of Architecture + Urban Planning
at the University of Michigan. The following
students have been awarded the scholarship:

John DeGraaf 1988
Matthew Petrie 1989
Elizabeth Govan 1990
Paul Warner 1991
Dallas Felder 1992
Eric Romano 1993
Charles Yoo 1994
Matthew Johnson 1995

acknowledgements

The College of Architecture and Urban Planning
is grateful for the generous support for the Raoul
Wallenberg Scholarship and Lecture which has been
provided by alumni, friends, and the Benard L. Maas
Foundation; for the assistance provided by the
International Institute of the University of Michigan in
publishing this document; and for the time and energy
so generously given by Nina and Daniel Libeskind.

In April 1995, 1000 copies of this book were printed and
given to the graduating class of 1995. Since then the
book has been made available in bookshops worldwide.
It went out of print in February 1996 on the same day
that Vincent Scully gave the 1996 Wallenberg Lecture.
We have reprinted 1000 copies in this second edition.

We heartily thank everyone who has embraced this
document so warmly.

PAGES	PHOTOGRAPH
13,15,17,18	Steven Gerrard & Elizabeth Govan / Studio Libeskind
22,23,28	Udo Hesse / Studio Libeskind
36	Eric Schall / Studio Libeskind
38L,39	Stefan Blach / Studio Libeskind
38R	Elizabeth Govan / Studio Libeskind
41	Manfred Beck
43	Leo Torri

Berg, Ruth, geb. | Berlin, Bella
Berg, Sabine | Berlin, Bella
Berg, Sally | Berlin, Erna, geb.
Berg, Sally | Berlin, Gertrud, g
Berta, geb. | Berg, Selma, geb. | Berlin, Hans
Berg, Selma, geb. | Berlin, Chle
Berg, Siegfried | Berlin, Ruth
Berg, Siegfried | Berliner, Jenny, g
Berg, Simon | Berlin, Hedwig
Berg, Simon | Berlin, Albin
Berg, Sophie, geb. | Berlin, Alfred
Berg, Walter | Berlin, Auguste
Berg, Werner R. | Berlin, Bernhard
Berg, Willi | Berlin, Denny
Berg, Willy | Berlin, Elli, geb.
Bergas, Frieda | Berlin, Erna, geb.
Bergas, Minna, geb. | Berlin, Erwin
Bergas, Wilhelm | Berlin, Eva, geb.
Berge, Emanuel | Berlin, Fanny, geb.
Berge, Ignatz | Berlin, Flora, geb.
Bergel, Josef | Berlin, Frieda, geb.
Bergel, Marianne | Berlin, Gertrud, g
Bergel, Rosa, geb. | Berlin, Gertrud,
Bergen, Albert | Berlin, Gudula
Bergen, Anton | Berlin, Gustav
Bergen, Charles | Berlin, Helene, g
Bergen, Clara S. | Berlin, Hilde, geb.
Bergen, Ella J. | Berlin, Hildegard
Bergen, Erna | Berlin, Horst
Bergen, Hedwig | Berlin, Ilse, geb.
Bergen, Max | Berlin, Irma
Bergen, Sally | Berlin, Jeannette
Bergen, Samuel | Berlin, Josef
Bergenstein, Klar | Berlin, Josef
Bergenthal, Elsa | Berlin, Kurt
Bergenthal, Ernst | Berlin, Leiser
Bergenthal, Mina | Berlin, Lotte
Bergenthal, Nane | Berlin, Malchen
Bergenthal, Regin | Berlin, Max
Berger, Adelheid | Berlin, Max
Berger, Adolf | Berlin, Paul
Berger, Adolf | Berlin, Regina R.
Berger, Adolf | Berlin, Ruth
Berger, Adolf | Berlin, Ruth, geb
Berger, Albert | Berlin, Sally
Berger, Alexande | Berlin, Selma, geb
Berger, Alfons | Berlin, Sigismund
Berger, Alfred | Berlin, Simon
Berger, Alfred | Berlin, Wilhelm
Berger, Alfred | Berlin, Wilhelmine
Berger, Amalie | Berliner, Edith
Berger, Amanda, | Berliner, Else
Berger, Anna, geb. | Berliner, Else
Berliner, Emmi, g
Berliner, Erna, geb
Berliner, Ernst
Berliner, Ester, g
Berliner, Eva